Insect World

Ants

by Mari Schuh

Ideas for Parents and Teachers

Bullfrog Books let children practice nonfiction reading at the earliest reading levels. Repetition, familiar words, and photo labels support early readers.

Before Reading

- Ask the child to think about ants. Ask: What do you know about ants?
- Look at the picture glossary together. Read and discuss the words.

Read the Book

- "Walk" through the book and look at the photos. Let the child ask questions. Point out the photo labels.
- Read the book to the child, or have him or her read independently.

After Reading

- Prompt the child to think more. Ask: Do you think one ant can survive by itself? What would it be like to lift food that is much heavier than you? Have you ever seen ants? What were they doing?

The author dedicates this book to Sam and Ben Krizek of Racine, Wisconsin.

Bullfrog Books are published by Jump!
5357 Penn Avenue South
Minneapolis, MN 55419
www.jumplibrary.com

Library of Congress Cataloging-in-Publication Data
Schuh, Mari C., 1975-
Ants / by Mari Schuh.
p. cm. -- (Insect world)
Summary: "This photo-illustrated book for early readers tells how ants find food. Includes picture glossary"--Provided by publisher.
ISBN 978-1-62031-050-2 (hardcover : alk. paper)
-- ISBN 1-62031-050-3 (hardcover : alk. paper) --
ISBN 978-1-62496-042-0 (ebook) -- ISBN 1-62496-042-1 (ebook)
1. Ants--Food--Juvenile literature. 2. Ants--Juvenile literature. I. Title. II. Series: Schuh, Mari C., 1975- Insect world.
QL568.F7S35 2014
595.79'6--dc23   2012039934

Series Editor   Rebecca Glaser
Book Designer   Ellen Huber
Photo Researcher   Heather Dreisbach

Photo Credits: Canstock, 1; Corbis, 6, 20–21, 23a; Dreamstime, cover, 11, 15, 18–19; Getty, 9; iStock, 3, 22, 24; Shutterstock, 5, 8, 10, 14, 23br; SuperStock, 16-17, 23tr; Veer, 4, 7, 12-13, 23bl

Printed in the United States of America at Corporate Graphics in North Mankato, Minnesota.
4-2013 / P.O. 1003

Table of Contents

Ants Look for Food

Ants are hungry little bugs.
They work hard to find food.

Ants live in groups
called colonies.

Colonies live
in nests.

Worker ants leave the nest.

They look for food.

Where is the food?
Is it here? Is it there?

antenna

Ants smell for food with their antennas.

The hungry ants
smell and smell.

They find bugs to eat.

They also find seeds
and leaves to eat.

The ants carry
food to the nest.

14

jaw

They use their strong jaws.

The ants leave
a trail of smells.

The trail leads more ants to the food.

More ants find food.

They carry food to the nest.

Chomp!
Chomp!

The hungry
little ants eat
in their nest.

Parts of an Ant

antenna
A feeler on an insect's head that ants use to smell and feel.

jaw
A part of the mouth used to bite, chew, carry, and dig.

leg
Ants have six legs, like all insects.

Picture Glossary

colony
A group of ants that live together.

trail
A path ants can follow to find more food.

nest
A home where ants live and raise young ants.

worker ant
A female ant that builds the nest, takes care of young ants, and looks for food.

Index

To Learn More

Learning more is as easy as 1, 2, 3.

1) Go to www.factsurfer.com

2) Enter "ant" into the search box.

3) Click the "Surf" button to see a list of websites.

With factsurfer.com, finding more information is just a click away.